This journal belongs to

Love ...
A gift from the Divine.
Like the gentle wings of a butterfly,
It dwells at the centre of our being.
Bright, pure, soft, fragile,
And yet infinite and eternal.
It is the seed of potential –
The heart of creation –
And to create is to know the Divine.

Love ...
It is a spark, a seed of light,
Planted within us when our soul was birthed.
Hold the spark of Love close,
Let it guide you to your true purpose,
Let it become a beacon to others –
Those whose light may falter.
Let it be your one true reason for being.

Love ...
A source of Strength,
A source of Hope,
A pathway to Divinity,
A path that leads you home.

– Ravynne Phelan